TWIN CITIES

TWIN CITIES

CAROL MUSKE-DUKES

PENGUIN POETS

PENGUIN BOOKS

Published by the Penguin Group
Penguin Group (USA) Inc., 375 Hudson Street, New York, New York 10014, U.S.A.
Penguin Group (Canada), 90 Eglinton Avenue East, Suite 700, Toronto, Ontario,
Canada M4P 2Y3 (a division of Pearson Penguin Canada Inc.)
Penguin Books Ltd, 80 Strand, London WC2R 0RL, England
Penguin Ireland, 25 St Stephen's Green, Dublin 2, Ireland (a division of Penguin Books Ltd)
Penguin Group (Australia), 250 Camberwell Road, Camberwell, Victoria 3124, Australia
(a division of Pearson Australia Group Pty Ltd)
Penguin Books India Pvt Ltd, 11 Community Centre, Panchsheel Park, New Delhi - 110 017, India
Penguin Group (NZ), 67 Apollo Drive, Rosedale, Auckland 0632, New Zealand
(a division of Pearson New Zealand Ltd)
Penguin Books (South Africa) (Pty) Ltd, 24 Sturdee Avenue, Rosebank,
Johannesburg 2196, South Africa

Penguin Books Ltd, Registered Offices:
80 Strand, London WC2R 0RL, England

First published in Penguin Books 2011

1   3   5   7   9   10   8   6   4   2

LIBRARY OF CONGRESS CATALOGING IN PUBLICATION DATA

Muske-Dukes, Carol, 1945–
Twin cities / Carol Muske-Dukes.
p.   cm.—(Penguin poets)
ISBN 978-0-14-311964-7
I. Title.
PS3563.U837T87   2011
811'.54—dc22   2011006709

Printed in the United States of America

Set in Garamond Premier Pro
Designed by Ginger Legato

This book is dedicated to my mother, Elsie Muske,
my sister, Michele Mueller, my daughter, Annie Muske-Dukes (Driggs)
and Diana Arterian, Laura Baudo Sillerman,
and Carol Olson Coote.

CONTENTS

TWIN CITIES

The Invention of Your Face

TWIN CITIES

It was the river that made them two—
The mills on one side,
The cathedral on the other.

We watched its swift currents:
If we stared long enough, maybe
It would stop cold and let us

Skate across to the other side.
It never froze in place—though
I once knew a kid, a wild funny

Girl, who built a raft from branches
(Which promptly sank a few feet out
From the elbow bend off Dayton's Bluff),

Who made it seem easy to believe.
We'd tried to break into Carver's Cave,
Where bootleggers hid their hot stash

Years after the Dakota drew their snakes
And bears on the rock walls and canoed
Inside the caverns. We knew there were

Other openings in the cliffs, mirroring
Those same rock faces on the other shore—
And below them the caves, the subterranean

Pathways underlying the talk and commerce,
The big-shot churches; undermining the false
Maidenliness of the convent school from which

My friend was eventually expelled for being
Too smart and standing up for her own smartness.
Too late, I salute you, Katy McNally. I think

That the river returned then to two-sidedness—
An overhung history of bottle-flash and drift.
I see you still: laughing as the lashed sticks

Sank beneath you, laughing as you did
That morning when the river lifted
Its spring shoulders, shrugging off

The winter ice, that thin brittle mirage—
Making you believe
We were all in this together.

TWO COASTS

I own them both.
Sometimes I wake up
In somebody else's night,
Somebody else's day.

I enjoy entering the lives
Of no one I know. You
Learn to live in transit,
Both trigger and safety.

I've been on the run since
He stopped drawing breath.
You want to be with me?
Boarding pass is my answer.

So every democracy of one's life
Has a little tyrant time. Perpetual
Motion, within my own shadow—
Away from me. I pledge allegiance

To it: Beauty, beauty. Skyscraper
Caverns, the gold riprap of heels
On pavement, silver Chrysler head-
Dress, jeweled fan of Korean fruits,

Times dropped like a straphanger on
The tracks. Then jet streams, operatic:
Desert-by-the-sea, back-lot, blue jaca-
Randa boulevards. A house afloat on

Earth, many houses rippling like the
Screen coming down in the screening
Room of someone I call Pal. O my pal
Is a vampire, sky-high on Sunset Blvd.,

Showing his choppers. Come to me,
Bloodlust, better yet good coffee on
Either side of the country. Blue ambassador,
I believe in myself. Like a law book studied in
Solitary: I want to be in as much as I want out.

SAN CLEMENTE

Beachcomber pier, rickety path over waves.
Blue neon martini glass. No red neon nipples.

No red neon tits. But staunch Republican
White stone promenade benches.

Carved words under bird-splat:
Everything in Moderation & Memories

Eternal as the Sea. Then the thirty-seventh
Prez, soul of checks & balances, pops up,

Beach glass. Shame, say the waves: *this,*
This. Continent's dream-stop, south of floating

Oil rigs, heavenly sweep of pitiless sea.
Dolphins, our leaping geniuses, are here

To save us, help us be kind. We are not.
The kind tide checks itself, balances, as

Sea rolls over in the salt plain. The criminal
Mind, uncaught, rolls jack-flat & over

Everything in Moderation. How poems depend
On fugitive causes. O fugitive, here is your

Sanctuary: *Memories Eternal as the Sea.*
I stood once with my love on a cliff

Near the old Del Coronado—watching
Hang gliders suspended in the sky, like

These blue neon dragonflies, floating spines
Alight . . . Joggers & shoppers ascend &

Descend. Look, says a lovely old woman:
The idea for escalators came from the waves.

THE INVENTION OF YOUR FACE

I was waiting when you came back from
Argentina—the summer you smuggled
Dulce de leche in your luggage. You talked

About the film: you'd discovered how
The proscenium shifted, haloing the body
In the camera gaze—and how you emerged

Through that fluid arch each frame. You'd
Missed me, you'd missed her: six years old
And suddenly shy in your presence. You

Spooned sweet milk paste from the tin into
Her cereal bowl—then let image after image
Appear for her through a camera lens you made

Of your hands, held like half-opened wings in the air.
She could see the great waterfall, Iguaçú, and miles
Of hardwood trees, called Breakers of the Axe,

Quebracho, as they swirled up in the Chaco—and one red
Horse galloping all by itself across the Pampa. I watched her
Changing expressions: I knew how many nights she'd gone

Searching for you, beyond the movable walls of a dream.
You showed her a little bird that sang in Patagonia wearing
A gaucho's hat and she ate sugar paste she barely tasted. She

Was a child; she took in whatever sweetness you
Provided—what sweetness there was in the world
That we could see. Silent, the two of us, staring at you—

We could never get past it: the invention of your face.

NEW YORK

This is the world in which we believe—
One planet evolving to boot-in-the-face
Harmony. People on the street? My

People. Buildings rise up: judges.
Take away each sight and sound,
You'd still have shimmer and beep

Recorded as this speeding unstoppable
Life. Subways, cathedrals, kite-clamor in the
Park. Horse-drawn models. Cult-sip:

Starbucks—cab downtown, cab uptown—
Fake sugar, sirens, drunk Library Lions, views
Of the river. Between two: a miracle.

One serious kiss is a City. One.
Chador-clad woman reading Calvino
On the A train. The One City, divisible.

I'll stand by the kiss & *Invisible Cities* that
Woman is reading. Pal, they are saving us.

Acceleration

CONDOLENCE NOTE: LOS ANGELES

The sky is desert blue,
Like the pool. Secluded.
No swimmers here. No smog—

Unless you count this twisting
Brushfire in the hills. Two kids
Sit, head to head, poolside,

Rehearsing a condolence note.
Someone has died: "Not an intimate,
Perhaps a family friend," prompts

The Manners Guide they consult.
You shouldn't say, *God never makes
Mistakes,* she quotes, snapping her

Bikini top. Right, he adds—you
Could just say, *He's better off,* or,
Heaven was always in his future.

There's always a better way to say,
We're sorry that he's dead—but
They're back inside their music now,

Pages of politeness fallen between them.
O do not say that the Unsaid drifts over us
Like blown smoke: a single spark erupts

In wildfire! Cup your hands, blow out
This wish for insight. Say, Forgive me
For living when you are dead. Say, Pardon

My need to praise, without you, this bright
Morning sky. It belongs to no one—
But I offer it to you, heaven in your future—

Along with silent tunes from the playlist,
The end-time etiquette book dropped
From the hand of the young sleeper.

It's all we have left to share, the book
Of paid respects, the morning's hot-blue
iPod, sunlit words on a page, black border.

RIVER ROAD

So you had your share of summer nights,
Cars braking fast along the river road.
The world was asleep yet alive with threat,
The high grieving sound of acceleration.

Beauty grew too fast, like your body:
Ungainly, unfaithful. Along the river road,
There were nodding lilacs. Every intersection
Dangerous. Your life dangerous, but you

Didn't know then how damage is made. Not
Just the flipped glittering chassis, spun apart
Into anecdote—but Night's notched-up velocity
Ascending through a blue reservoir of scent.

No, to remember the inevitable in terms
Of engaged, disengaged, gear to gear, one
Heightening judgment, is to forget that back
Then the worst happened each time it happened.

What was speaking loud over the figure on the dash—
That was God or not God—something flashing past
Each roadside presence: statue after gesturing statue
Trying to reverse your belief in imagination

As the opposite of fate. Imagine a speed
At which you could make what was happening
Not be true, a speed at which you could bargain
For it: that you, on fire, from this minute forward,

Could be somebody else.

BOY

They called me "boy" in Kashmiri,
Because they had no other word for what I
Appeared to them to be. Taller by a half foot—
Gawky in my rolled jeans and cap—they

Chose to look away from my small breasts and
Voice-lilt and rename me in the lexicon of sex.
The shikari—mysterious, wizened, in loose turbans—
Were our guides, up the mountain and through

The wall of white water. They linked arms with us
And waded us through to the high still pools above,
Where we'd cast for trout. They stepped in and out
Of Allah as we climbed, in sun and shade, singing

His name. We were miles above Srinagar and two
Hundred miles from China and the finned bodies
Were swift under the surface. The shikari pointed:
Budd gaard-e! Big fish! Then they murmured

Their one word for me and it was not *sister* or
Daughter: I was naked face; twenty-seven, a rebel,
I thought. Therefore they made me their oversight.
Had they not looked away from me as they spoke,

Had it been otherwise, they would have heard it,
Above the peaks—the clear unwavering call, a
Command to rip my cap away, to pick up stones.
To separate my face from my face, stripping the

Veil from a hook of air, holding it over my breath till
I gasped like a fish, till I was a pair of eyes on a plate,
That body the world wishes both to savor and destroy.

HEROINE

Then Jane says: there is an invisible thread between
Our hearts that can never be broken. And Rochester
Goes on acting tormented, doomed soon to re-
Negotiate his own contract with the visible. So

The happy ending relies, as always, on varieties
Of comeuppance: Jane's class avenged, Rochester
Humbled and sightless, the mad "colonial" wife
Setting fire to the rafters, the little kid coquette

Traipsing off into oblivion or reader amnesia, leaving
A faint scent of wisteria on the page. Unlike Jane,
who leaves no recognizable scent, she wears
Self-effacement like the startling whiff of a nun's habit:

Laundered dreams. Targetless, her neutered wild
Look, even meeting Rochester's black piratical gaze,
Refusing her own image in the glass. Her little set chin,
Her eyes-down dowryless style, that hurt implicit power.

Except for the matter of the thread, the breath-colored
Filament linking two hearts with pretty much nothing
In common. The thread pulses like a Brontë umbilical,
Which it is. We are reminded once again that its length

Is infinite, its connection eternal. Though not, finally,
For the two sexes; rather, woman to woman, beyond
Class or aptitude. Like the clean path of the flare,
Shot and ascending across latitudes, against satellite

Winds, visible limits, against judgment itself—
Into our global-posited pop rocket of Love Me,
Love Me—O blind and careless Master!

CAMILLA

*—Virgil invented Camilla, leader of the Volscian army of
women, dedicated by her father to Artemis.*

My father first threw me across water,
An infant, pinned to a javelin. In the warrior
Dream of the risen body, heaven is a precinct

Of sweetmeats and concubines. My heaven
Was constant flight. He threw me skyward,
So that I would never doubt the will's fierce transit.

Fate was another kind of fate. What I took to be
Divine momentum—flung from his hand and sped
Onward with the hawk's guidance—turns out to be

Merely a weapon's trajectory. Pity the weapon,
The missile locked on doom—launched and accelerating

In the name of the fool illusions: perfect human aim,
                                God-given prophecy.

REQUEST RADIO

Call up and ask for them—
Oldies like "All Glory to the Fetus"
"I'm Not a Witch, I'm You!" Or get
Down with "Nuke Ground Zero Mosque."

Or other tacky favorites:
The heart's nonstop mimicking
Of what hurts. Sound of war—

Sing along with the Morality Police,
Beating a woman for a shown inch
Of wrist. What's that called again?

Each one of us an Auto-Patriot,
Hero to himself, to her spotlit
Ongoingness. Then a gangsta signal

From the Not-You. Someone else's
Play-list. *What says the soul?*
That's the way poets talk.

Here are the five tyrant senses—
Set on refusing the mind's deep dumb
Resuscitative kiss. That's how poets
Talk. How does that go again?

Let me hear just once more the Kismet
Jingle of the dead lover's breath. Instead
I keep getting these voices broadcast

In the name of corporate rap . . . You know,
Victory in the Pyrrhic lyric not the scat-
Madrigal of shower acoustics:

O You and You and I failing in love, failing in love . . .
          Hearing it first on Death's request radio.

CRACK THE WHIP

If you were the very last one on the line
Rotating round the axis, you were a kid
Winging it, hunkered down, scarf flying,

Ice-blind. Your blades drawing sparks
On the rink's surface as they spun out—
As you, spinning out, still held on tight

To the next up, the one fighting now
To let go of your hand, the centrifugal
Pull you'd become—while on the other

Side of the mirror, your twin fought
The same fight. Around the piano,
During wind and rain, the bright faces

Sang, out of tune, "Where Does the Old
Year Go?" But we know: the skater, shot
At last from orbit by the whip's final crack,

Keeps spiraling (the light-swept faces
One by one go dark) or rolling over and over,
In snow, staring up at the distant glitter, still

Hearing the circling cries. There is a crow,
Always a crow. Where Does the Old Year Go?
Center-wise: what becomes of the big shots

Revving the engines? Best & worst, passionate intensity.
Face-to-face with the whirling god desiring Nothing's
Blue accelerating buzz . . .

No past when the whip snaps: you're new again.
The skater, flung off, lone mitten. So much depends on that snap!
The tether is severed; we're solo, still—where the year turns, on us:

Solstice in a snowy wood.

Pierce County

TWIN CITIES II

I come from Twin Cities, where
The river between, surging, stands.

I believed once that what I called desire
Flowed in that confluence between twins,

Capitol and rapids. I come from Twin
Cities: dark and light. Still the river

Was dammed, managed for miles above the locks:
Even at the source where some god's mouth opened

And what we called holy thundered in every synonym.
Two mirrored cities: their symmetry invented as my own

Present, twinned to a past to which it is now forever
Subordinate. Twinned to a future, stunned in its

White eclipse. So they killed the white foxes,
Brought their pelts to market in the one named

For the Saint pierced by lightning. The richer
Sister prospered on threshed tons near the shared

Slaughterhouse. If the snow grew steeped in blood,
They raised a Court. But the Ojibway said no-one

Out-thinks the two-in-one. The river was dammed,
The moon afloat, an animal face, in the crossed

Ambivalent tales of the French and the Squareheads,
Beyond those of the suffering ancients. Gold domes down-

Town, imitating the gold clouds of the Sioux, vision-figures
Who doubled and doubled but remained apart. A single

Mind, forever unable to refuse its overstatement: blood
On snow, the gnawed bars of the trap, crack after crack

In the courthouse floor. And one irrefutable truth after another—
Obliterated by the irrefutable dual: City and City and

River and river of this, my Ever-Dividing Reflection.

TO A SOLDIER

—Lt. Col. Edward Ledford

Imagine it: a world away, Autumn.
Leaves scattering, but not in fiery
Effusion, like the red/gold sentinels

Of the Smokies or north of Boston.
A world away: not enough Fall to
Make a cliché, the one we love about

The season's redemptive powers, its
Dazzling imitation of death, the gold & blood—
Colors. In the desert, in the cities of armaments—

You tell me the leaves die without turning—
Without color, they die. Without a sign
Of how it ended, the season, how it was lost to us.

BEIRUT, 1983

The baby was lifted in its flowing shroud
And carried through the red-lit streets,
Floating above the raised fists of men
In headcloths. The wrapped body a cloud,
Pall burden so light, it seemed weightless
Crowning the mad cortege. That shape

Once living in her arms—that shape
I mirrored, newborn at my breast. Shroud
So light it became an unsupportable weight,
As *TIME* fell open before me. I saw the street
Going up in flames, but couldn't see, in the cloud
Of fire, her face. What dark veil or wall of men

Hid her? *TIME* opened to the images of men.
I couldn't see her; just her grief, unraveling shape,
White streaming from the breast. That cloud
Of chants, bitter witness to the small shroud
Held high. She stood away from the fiery street—
The monument of her shadow, that weighted

Absence. Who shrugged the machine gun's weight,
Wrenched from her the stopped heart? Which man
Explained their intent? Did she cry out, over street
Sounds unheard, as they lifted the bloodied shape
From her embrace? Sirens, miles of shrouded
Windows, drone of a bomber above the clouds—

Hearts: flaming paint on the fuselage. A cloud
Of dust blurring the camera lens. Drifting weight
Of dark. Night shoulders the remains of day, shroud-
Lit moon. Then *TIME* opened, with men
Carrying the future, its lit fuse, that infant shape
Held up like a bomb spinning over bombed streets.

Nothing to say: mother, reader of *TIME*. Streets
I'd never walked, people and cries, a cloud
Of broken stares, hovering over her nursing shape,
Bent, clinging to the small lifeless weight.
I knew her milk still flowed, unsummoned. Men
With guns stood at her door, opening the shroud.

PIERCE COUNTY

Something in her wants to give up, just weep, but no.
Because she has just been told that her father is dead,
She stops listening to the false chorus in her head—
There from the cradle, telling her they made the world

Safe. Now just her mother's voice, just the one voice,
On the phone with Death & Co. Now the two of them:
They are survivors, but on a planet newly-made, where
The atmosphere is contradiction, where in a reversal of

Gravity he weighs nothing and drifts upward as
The two of them, lifting their arms of stone, try
To pull him back. Her mother's new voice of stone
On the telephone with men who have taken him away,

Taken away his body, refusing to relinquish it
Or allow them to fly to him, so they can push up against
The stopped heart in his chest, breathe into the mouth
That was once his speaking mouth. They have taken

His body away in another city, another state, where
This morning he was an actor in a movie. They have
Made a grave error; they have defied the script
Written in ancient characters. It will be a day

Before the desecration is headlined—but
Just hours too late. Tomorrow his body will
Be opened unlawfully by strangers, before courts
Can intervene, before they can defy time & stand

At his side. It is a crime against the dead, against
The beauty and strength of her father. In school
They are reading *Antigone*—she knows the dead
Have rights, the dead are entitled to great tenderness.

Too late, the lawyer, too late, the good doctor.
Her mother is trying to reason with the Coroner,
Who allows no family in the basement chambers,
Where the dead are held hostage. On Earth,

In his county, he can do this. On the new planet,
She thinks, I am Antigone, pouring the sand
Over his body, shielding him against the black
Gravity. I am Antigone and I rise from the abyss

Over your petty office: Pierce County Medical
Examiner's Office, Tacoma, Washington.
I rise on my stone wings—John Howard,
Look up. At your last breath in your wolf-trap

Terminus, may all you wronged & their own
Surround you, your heart pounding like fists
On a closed door. Beyond that door, we
Could have made him David again, in water,

In burial cloths. In this bad planetary light,
Look at the face of Antigone: you who made him
A corpse rigid in a steel drawer. In Pierce County,
He became not David by your hand. Look at me:

Not David but tagged meat, bones strewn in
A desert, a trough of blood, arms & legs
In a bag sent home from a lost war—my
Father's body. Look at my face, the face

Of his daughter, as you turn to the wall—
This is Antigone's wall, which you built,
Stone by stone. Which you will dismantle,
Stone by stone, in your eternal Bureau of Death.

THE GO-BETWEEN

He was not the one who had died,
Yet it became clear to me when I
Touched his body that its hunger was
Identical to that other hunger, its face

In extremity so like the one Death had
Erased. Death had bled the quick heart
In that familiar breast, closed forever
The once-only eyes. Yet here too was

The other singularity, the heat he'd turned
Against me, the specific face of indifference,
His hand across my mouth. What was it I was
Meant to understand? That his mind still clung,

Married to its bed? For what had he bartered?
The body, intact again—unknowable as before,
As in any failed premise of union? Brute-accurate:
It held me, in exactment, face-to-face with the man

In the bed, twin effigy. My body sent back, sent ahead.
Double emissary before whom I kneeled, eager. Not
Once did I ask it why I was allowed to recognize this
Passion, unselved, recognize one inhuman face

Gradually eclipsing another. Why was I permitted
To hold it shouting in my arms—conscious, battered,
Wild orphaned life—so filled with defeat, so damaged,
I wondered if the gods under the earth had chosen him—

Who'd crossed their River, jettisoned Memory
Like all the rest—to come harmed, ecstatic, back?

TWIN TREE

A tree divided. It grew like that—
Its slender trunk suddenly forking,

Lifting up from the crux in two Shiva arms—
As if it had come to a crossroads and split

The way twins unpeel from one another
In the womb. Two from one, it reached up

And flourished this way—it topped thirty feet
As its thick dark glossy leaves, half-folded like

Paper boats, kept the nubs of coming pears
Hidden then dangling. Avocado, avocado.

I held you in my hand as a big wrinkled pit,
Propped you (as I'd been taught once by a lover

Who was trouble) with four toothpicks over a glass
Filled with water—till the tiny white filament inside

Your worried seed slowly let itself down into the
Clear transparency, while sprouting above into a

Green feasible stem. I transplanted those floating roots,
The top-heavy shoot, after weeks, then waited till it

Reached out at last—growing fast in both directions,
Down into dirt, up into the sky over the backyard. When

It twinned, climbing upward, I stopped my husband,
Standing hard by with a shears, from pruning it back

Into one: *The only way it would survive*, he said. But
It doubled skyward into the single tree at the top—

A hermaphrodite, as it had to be to make fruit. So
Many alligator pears, summer after L.A. summer! We

Filled baskets with the abundance of the you
And you: the fruit of two separate flowerings

From one quick hesitation. Till days after David died,
When clumsy workmen, digging a trench, severed your

Taproot. I saw the white exposed arteries they'd chopped clean
With their spades. I stood beside you weeping, trying to hold

Your heart together with my hands at the fork where you'd
Leaned apart, then towered. You were my love, conflict tree—

Tough-skinned, the rich light-green flesh beneath. Avocado,
They killed you. When we sold the house, you were a cut stump.

WIDOWS

On Halloween Eve my friend & I
Sit at a table draped in sunset red.
Grapes, pears & pomegranates—

A small bountiful harvest piled
Between us: two glasses of wine.
We are widows. We are women

Of grief but we wear no black.
A wire halo sits on my head,
Tall rabbit ears attached. My

Friend pops on her gorilla mask
Each time pirates, vampires,
Unicorns or terrifying insurance

Executives knock, demanding
Sweet passage. On the table sits
A flickering flat candle my friend

Found in a dusty joke shop: a skeleton
Lying in a coffin with a wick burning
Between its legs where his family jewels,

As we say, spark up. It is good to
Think, sipping wine, how Love always
Has a beginning and sometimes no end.

But Passion, that infinite practical joke,
Is another matter, surviving in spite of us,
Flaming up again & again in the presence

Of endings. The lit wick diminishing, the
Handfuls of sweets vanishing—and this
Trick and quiver of the unforgettable Once-

Body, spending to ashes. Burning hot
In its toy crypt—burning all night before
Us, before our widows' eyes.

MARRIAGE

Till death we navigate the unbridgeable river
       Between spouse and spouse.

Between together and two: a torrent.
What lies just left of her as she strokes his bent head—

It pours over them. The mind begins to row—
Needing never alone. Little raft/self

On its own currents. The river has no desire
To be known. Rises anonymous till the voices of the drowned

Wake her. Ha-ha. Sun is not yet up, no smell of bread
Or coffee. This is when the mind resists all metaphors,

Gets wise. Ha-ha. Let it go—the rudderless joy of
Knowing there is nothing downstream. Count: two.

CROWS

They were not the messengers I'd expected.
Late at night, I stared at the moonlit photograph:
The bird's furtive yellow gaze bent back over its
Wing, beak clamped on a gold wedding band.

At dawn, I woke to my wedding rings beside me
In the bed, next to my naked hand. Thief! That
Ragged caw, turning one hand against the other.
A body winging over the temple of change—gold

Mouths mouthing the terrible—Vows: I spoke them.
Crows circle, harden the bond. See how
The high piracies of the sky turned imperative—
Sanctioned by me, my dream:
                    I stole the past that willingly from myself.

Suttee Goddess

SUTTEE

Some go willingly,
Some resist.

The fire in which his body burns
Lights into her thin negligee, her hair—

One way or another: she comes back
From that pyre as ash.

Sati, that nonstop goddess, ignited herself
Like a lighter thumbed open—

Flame like a slit throat—
Gilt-black: the copper-red avenger.

He wants to make love to you one last time.
A widow I know made herself into a nerve

Kite: up, up, in smoke. Because he'd blown
Himself away and left her with a fury at him

She could never express. O she burns, burns,
In her own bones. What good are the earth's

Rickety steps hacked into the hillside? Ascend,
Ascend, little sheep. He loves me, he loves me not.

I try to stay a step ahead of the flames,
But he's so fast, like his hand across my face,

On my throat—the hem catches, then the stitching.
His profile floats up from the raised platform—

One gold ring, two: molten. I had that same dream,
Sati. But now I swear, I will not go willingly.

DAWN MASS, PAST

Unstoppable courier, no news in her pack, she
Plunges through the new drifts, opening no path.
It's dawn and twenty below, the Holy Spirit
Flickers in a street-lamp's lantern, turns to
Black glass as she passes: nine and fanatical,

Blue-legged, in high boots. *Who made the cold?*
Satan made the cold, said the bad catechism.
God was improvisational, less dependable:
Glassed-in orchids *here,* a tornado *there.*

Satan burned slowly along his great spine
Of ice, turned away, meditating, as the sky
Grew light. Thus cold was made cold by pure thought,
Implacable, progressive as the idea of Self . . .

Who made you? God made me. But Satan made
The deep facade of longing—Satan made this day
Wherein she stands alone on the snowy steps,
Waiting for a sign, before her mittened hand

Shatters the sheer thin surface, half-formed
Over the still water, blessed in its marble font.

OUR KITTY

She is swinging in a contraption above the heads
Of the audience,
      Reflected in the glass lamps on the tables.

She sits in one of those fin de siècle gilded sleighs
Hung from the ceiling
      By braids of sparkling hemp.

Here come all the text-creepers, shuffling in
To talk about *meta-agency & fluid locality:*
      Reclaiming the anus.

The ceiling is hammered tin, alight and jumping
With her shadow,
      Cast upward by the table lamps.

As she swings, she rubs herself, adjusts herself
In the seat so she
      Can be seen through the see-through bottom.

Pink cheeks has Kitty. A pop-open camisole. Mother
Is striking her
      Name from the family bible. But

She has to eat, does Kitty! Kitty, so petite & incautious
That all the critic-onanists quietly
      Get off on the thought: *envaginate!*

Perhaps she is the sweetest whore
  Of Imagination, pole dancer Muse—
    They valorize, *a starkly gendered sex worker.*

So the century goes on, just like the earlier
  Centuries:
    The dream of body parts floating

Above cigar smoke. In other words, *more war. More fucked.*
Kitty inspires interiority:
    Think about triage: (In other words: Me first!)

Poet or text-creeper—
  Who should be saved?

The poet in her brain tourniquet?
The academics waving their death warrants for words?

    Someone in a lowrider hearse knows
The price of this ending. Plus those boards of trustees
  In the back with their bodyguards—

And the poet bleeding all over the tablecloths—
Who wants to be John Keats?
  (Well, the poems, yes. But not the death!)

Now they hear Kitty as she
  Coughs loudly. I'm Keats, she gasps.

I'm John Fucking Keats, returned in Kitty's body!
Forlorn, she cries, *forlorn!*
    But they refuse to listen to her

As she swings, pale and beautiful, glittering, above them,
Holding out her
        Living hand, warm, capable—as ever, untaken.

ADDICTS

Monsters, all of them. The ones who
Gave one life, the ones who take life

Back. The big bloodbath: Family
Romance and hot woe, the Mom

Who shoots up, the Dad who flashes—
Sex fiends, hand-cranked snakes-in-

The-grass, uncles, aunts, boys & girls,
Gay & straight. Rocketing up and down

The twelve steps to confront the big
Mocked sad-as-shit Self, mirrored

In the Times by the Depts. of War
& Good Works: breathing life

Back into those we need to kill
To restore Peace. There will be

Heaven-sent ideologies: every
Religion tweaked & sold like crystal

Meth. In the heart, in the vein—
What passes for Populism is

Set forth by the guy on the Internet
Who wants to be eaten alive. Buddy,

We all want to be eaten alive—isn't
That finally It? You, me, a bottle of

Château d'Yquem, some techno-
Lute, Catullus's words piped in, just to

Keep us honest—and then, the Donner
Party all over again, but by choice this time.

OUR LADY OF PEACE HIGH SCHOOL

Her name unfurled above us, wind-tight banner
Over a barricade. We sang her praises in Glee—
But there was no statue erected to her: no votives

In the hallways, where we were struck silent
(One laugh, one demerit) in passing. But flowers lay
At the plaster feet of St. Philomena, though her head

Was covered later in a hood of deep annihilating habit-
Colored shadow, at news she'd been a hooker
In ancient Rome, not a Blessed Half-Canonized.

More blossoms at the feet of St. Joseph, Holy Cuckold,
His surprised eyes popping from half-dollar-size sockets.
We served the nuns: our leaders, our love affairs. Their

Waist-slung rosary beads threatening us with mild
Affection, the way a diplomat who wants peace, but
Knows he must hurt everyone in the name of peace,

Might threaten. Lady of Shock & Awe or Victim of
Shallot, adrift in her graffiti'd barge? Sky-walker atop
Our globe, flattening Eve's snake under her starry feet?

Though she had no plinth in the corridor,
I still hoped to glimpse her as she'd once been—
Infinitely patient, weary of explaining all,

But beautiful. Arnaut Daniel's Lady, Pound's—
Old bitch gone in the teeth. Still, an age built on
Her Beginning. Who would give up peace for beauty?

Those thousand ships, churning toward it, it.
Do I have to be beautiful, I wondered, if I only
Want peace? I was that clueless yet vain.

Why couldn't I be Our Lady of Sez Who?
Lady of Kiss My Ass? I never asked, not
For those years of the chanted trivium: Latin,

Ancient History, Warfare & the Unities. Those
Were her colors up on the battlements, on
Our girl-bodies. Blue & Gold, sky & booty.

But no witness, no one to drive us, pure products
Of that emptiness, that profound & holy name.

KAY

S.F. State, a little seminar. Her
House in the Haight. Talked only
Of Revolution, that razor gaze,

Man Ray head-tilt. Talked only
Jail & student marches. Later:
Her poems on mountain gentian.

Never answered about the past.
I came once to sit with her &
My Thesis—she drifted back

To the spotlit ruins. To Lucia,
Joyce's mad daughter, who Joyce
Said had dreams "just like his own."

But Jung allowed how Joyce dived
In and resurfaced, how Lucia fell
Into dreams "and drowned." She

Leaned back, entering some foyer
Of her fine prose—

O to live again
In the perilous precincts of Lucia,

Kept afloat by one's unsubmerged
Mind! Described once as a blade,
Her body, her insight. From outside:

Tart smell of grass, a speed freak,
Shouting. Her voice gone, she slept,
And I waited at the feet of Kay Boyle.

HOME-BOYS: BABY & ME (a Sapphic)

Ex-gang members. Drive-by days over. Zero
Tattoos, tagging. Sippy cups, hoodies. Baby
Daddies gather, stubble-cheeked, holding infants.
Rock-a-bye Central.

Awkward former enemies, rubbing elbows,
Slow-bounce babies: parachute cradle. X-nay
Gangsta language—A is for Apple, only.
Alphabet shakedown.

Toddler nap-time. Whispering pretty teenage
Mothers. Foxy counterparts, purple lipstick,
Dreamy iPod lullaby, off-key. Next up:
Diapering for two.

Outside: L.A. traffic jam, backfires, smog-red
Sunset. Inside: recipes, meal plans, flowered
Hand-wipes, homemade. Tabletop mirror mirrors
Pick Up Stix, Windex.

HATE MAIL

You are a whore. You are an old whore.
Everyone hates you. God hates you.
He pretty much has had it with all women—

But, let me tell you, especially you. You like
To think that you can think faster than
The rest of us—hah! We drive the car

In which you're a crash dummy! So
Why do you defy our Executive Committee
Which will never cede its floor to you? If a pig

Flew out of a tree & rose to become
A blimp—you would write a poem
About it, ignoring the Greater Good,

The hard facts of gravity. You deserve to be
Flattened by the Greater Good—pigs don't
Fly, yet your arrogance is that of a blimp

That has long forgotten its place on this earth.
Big arrogance unmoored from its launchpad
Floating free, up with mangy Canadian honkers,

Up with the spy satellites and the ruined
Ozone layer, which is, btw, caused by your breath,
Because you were born to ruin everything, hacking

Into the inspiration of the normal human ego.
You are not Queen Tut, honey, you are not
Even a peasant barmaid, you are an aristocrat

Of trash, landmine of exploding rhinestones,
Crown of thorns, cabal of screech-bats!
I am telling you this as an old friend,

Who is offering advice for your own good:
Change now or we will have to Take Measures—
If you know what I mean, which you do—

& now let's hear one of your fucked-up poems:
Let's hear you refute this truth any way you can.

PARROT

You'd sit quietly and suddenly the Parrot would shout,
"Death is the Mother of Beauty!"—and then she'd

Nod and eat a burrito. She was taciturn, but if you
Pushed her, she'd become fiery and cry: "My life
Had stood, a Loaded Gun!" and fan her feathers.

What do you have to offer that is more inventive
Than the Parrot's glittering discourse? What do you
Have to say that could not be topped by: "The world

Is too much with us," "Sunset and evening star,"
"We real cool," & "They feed they lion"—
Or, "Whose woods these are I think I know"?

I think I know, the Parrot protests. I honestly think
I know, but I am so tired of squawking the same
Profound shimmering insights—& nobody listening!

Scout

SCOUT

The dog must have run for miles.
Messenger from nowhere.
Fireworks lit up the harbor.

White dog in dark outside my house.
So long not wanting my life. Artillery sounds
As the sky lit. Twin to my own white "rescue"—

Back when I had a family. Same wolf-face—
At my door, soaking wet and panting terror.
Scout, said his tag. Owner's name, numbers

I called, but all that night no one came for Scout.
He paced on my floor, stood sentry by the pool
Staring back at me. Fireworks lit up the harbor.

At last he slept by my bed, white dog in dark.
Morning: the phone lit up—last night
His owner had drowned alone in her pool.

Before those eyes. Her eyes on his.
The rumors later that she hadn't wanted to live.
He'd come, emissary, to me. That was illusion.

He had tried to save her. That was hope.
Such evidence that she loved him.
Tags, numbers—strategies to survive.

But the merciless dictates of hope.
The merciless dictates of the message.
She, wading into tinted water. His shadow,

The harbor lighting up. Then, in deeper darkness—
White dog, running for miles.

THE PAINTER RECONSIDERS HIS CANVAS

—For Eric Fischl

The brush moves blue through a wedding—
Till no wedding is left. The bride, spared,
Smokes her Lucky near a white marble fountain.

A stroke and the bride begins to resemble Ghandi,
The veil falling to her feet. She stares as she is re-
Made: everyone wants to live. He sees through

Her to a mountain, then through the mountain to
A scrim of ash, fire-lit—then through that too,
So that the saint, half-clad pacifist, can rise up

In a bride's form. He marries what the eye desires
With what it naturally erases. Re-emerging slowly
Through smoke, the bride lives, though she half-surfaces.

If he is holy, she is closer
To God, who keeps vanishing through her. If
A woman wears a veil she is sacred—or burning up.

Hands unravel within her gaze. Meanwhile
The brush is flickering, restless. Meanwhile they will
Be brought to the surface or left clear as breath.

Because the eye sees we are made and
Remade in the mind of another mind.
So the fountain rises high into the sky because

We recognize our galaxy but know nothing of her
Exile. The woman is veiled, the man, separate
In his cloth and sandals, spins: now a warlord. The

Fountain pours its blue division over each of them—
The woman, the man—a reflection
Upon which to stand. But the paint covers

Them now: war, peace, sudden brushstrokes.
They are seen—seen together—then brushed out.

THE GRIEF GAME

Some say that all elegies are mirrors—
But I say I'd rather imagine Catullus

Ranting in his brim-back ninth-inning cap:
That you're never going to feel better

About losing the one person you never
Wanted to lose. Habeas corpus. But face

It. We're all players of the Grief Game,
So ante up! Two dead friends are trumped

By one late spouse (and suicides are wild—
Like Dead Man's Hand: take all). Grandma

& Grandpa are lowball vs. one baby at
Birth or old enough to text . . . You begin

To tell your tale of loss and they start in
On theirs: the friend with brain cancer

Whom you never liked—how can one
Cupped match rival your Eternal Flame?

I knew a widower who cheered at
The news of a plane shrieking out

Of the sky one day after he'd buried her—
Or the widow who told me she'd

Happily see her sympathetic friends
Slaughtered, if that brought Hubby back.

Tell me, Catullus, on what flat stone
Do we barter for their remains &

Sell out the stakes? We say we'd
Bring them back, one by one, by shiny

Hearse-train or that single black chariot?
Or maybe not at all—if we had to snuff

Our own candles-in-the-wind as collateral?
Nights praying he'd walk through the door,

Shouting, Hi, I'm home! But wait! At the
Cost of you, Indispensable You, facedown

In the pantry, stiff! Life tries to imitate
Art, and art Death—but there's that flat

Stone, in this desert here, where, alone, within a
Heartbeat: we are absolutely nothing to each other.

COLD LIGHT

Vermont summer, years back—
In the buggy country house
Of the cracked ex-shrink (from

Whom we'd rented on a whim—
I lay awake, across the creaky
Bed from your turned back,

Staring at the tear-shaped
Flasher on the answering machine,
Avid repeating green: *two calls.*

Till through the broken screen,
A lit-up blinker of a bug fumbled
In & found, blind luck, that green

Erogenous wink, made of (he
Seemed to think) the same
Cold light filling his lamp-shaped

Privates. He hunkered down
Beside his throb, flickering
In synch with her nonstop

Non-response on the console.
How could he not see that she
Was a man-made incandescence

& despite the firefly byplay of
Their radiance, they would never
Mate—not made, as they were, poor

Glimmerings, to consummate cold love?

MIRROR

The first independent act I managed as a haunted
Kid was to lift the heavy round antique mirror
I'd found in the attic and hang it from a nail

Pounded into my bedroom plaster. It shuddered,
Askew but holding—as I peered at myself:
Ugly, I thought, but for the first time, visible.

But my father stood in the doorway, framed
And pointing within the glass, predicting it, the
Damn downfall, explosion into a thousand pieces!

Now in my sixty-third year, the mirror graces
My bedroom wall. In its depths each man who
Stood behind me in reflection, all disappeared.

And the image—shattered, unshattered—visible.

THE ARMY YOU HAVE*

You sent up Rumsfeld—the way he
Equivocated in front of the troops in Iraq.
You made a poem of that failure and the fury
Of the soldiers, unarmored, unsafe—

Soldiers, unsafe? Call up Henry Reed,
The Brit airman poet, figuring those fears
Back when they still had battlefronts.

Naming of Parts: a rifle, put together
In a garden—the garden's "silent eloquent
Gestures"—in a world gone out of order.

How does a world go out of order? You
Tell me now, a thousand thousand miles away,
In Kabul, which you say is "safe"—

O tell me how words can go out of order—
The cartoon-faced thug-commander knows:

As you know, you go
To war
With the Army you have.

*Found poem assembled by Lt. Col. Edward Ledford (U.S. Army) from remarks by
Secretary of Defense Donald Rumsfeld, speaking to troops in Iraq. (With added last
lines.)

They're not the Army
You might want or wish
To have at a later time.

And if you think about it,
You can have all the armor
In the world
On a tank
And a tank
Can be blown up.

It is something you
Prefer not to have to use,
Obviously, in a perfect world,

Which in your case,
You have not got.

AZTEC DANCERS

My beautiful daughter flies through
The student newspaper office—then
Straight out the window to the balcony—

Camera on her shoulder, bold,
Her bright hair a shout. I call to her,
But she is filming the Aztec dancers

Below in the quad. I can hear the drums,
But cannot see the green flashing quetzal feathers,
Each pause and extended step. She calls them back to me:
Birds, drums, shimmering breastplates. Be careful—

But the drums are so loud she cannot hear me.
The crowd is cheering below. For one second
She looks back, the camera still trained on the quetzal
Shape below, *like a great bird forming here*—

She shouts, closing then opening her father's eyes.

GREEN RIVER CEMETERY

"Grace to be born and to live as variously as possible"
from Frank O'Hara's epitaph

O his epitaph is happy—
A small shoal of grace: *To be*
Born and to live variously—

A leap from the stark head-
Stone Jean chose—the blank
Last page in her lightning

Style. Late friends, they lie
In Green River, near where I off
& on live. Yet dying takes us far

& variously, as Frank says, his
Tablet lying flat, like a toy
Shield cast aside, its carved

Words brightening in sun.
Sometimes I come here with
Awed poets who spend time

Among the names, loitering—
As on the page. Waiting
For a phrase, lighting up

A smoke: a touch of white
Space between characters.
All around us are the wild

Plots of artists: painted boulders,
Signed mirrors. But the poets
Kneel down to read: *Frank*

O'Hara, Jean Stafford. Re-
Member Me, urges each epitaph.
Remember yourself—walking

Here among dreams & signatures,
Awake for a little while, biding
Like a caught breath, then drifting
On the grounds of Green River.

STAND-UP DELUSIONS

First

She invented a man in a novel who died the way
Her husband happened to die, later. What might
Be called coincidence. Or, as one critic put
It, mercilessly, "No sooner said!" Who
Believes a writer writes the world into being?

Second

In the restaurant I face her pious smile—
Stuck soul who denies global warming
Also a woman's right to her own body.

I don't mention those near-lives I decided
Against in clinics, facing smiles, sunflowers.

On the dying planet, we are seated. Heads bow
Over plates of baby shrimp, beef, wall-eyed pike.

Third

O Late Style of Fire: I was your lover in
That "apricot-tinted chemise" in my Gramercy
Park flat, bright winter City. In fact, it was
A camisole. Peach silk. & I didn't banish you.

We were, as you wrote, "in love," inconveniently.
Even at your father's death, that fiery forbidden
Given. So American, that collision of infidelity &
Longed-for innocence. Those "bright green eyes
That widened" at the airport—those were my eyes.

We stood at the gates to your father's silent lit City.
Those drifting Spring nights in Iowa, another city,
Saying goodbye in my doorway—I kissed
The doorframe, desiring you to go. Reading Pavese

Later: "Death will come and will have your eyes."
Green & widening. So you were banished after all,
And the gates opened, but on a city so ridiculously tragic you
Hang there still, laughing, hilarious, hands in your pockets.

Watching the rafters, beams, the doorframes blaze upward. Spring:
Widening spell of ash. Too late now, Linnet, to show up at my address.

Fourth

GG wrote, "Hatred is a failure of imagination"—yet to be hated by
A true poet is to be perfectly imagined. For example, Mandelstam's
Fatal stand-up image—Stalin's "cockroach mustache." "We live

Without feeling the country beneath our feet." We moon-walk above
Our graves—we poets, pals of irrelevancy, O we are least
Imagined as real. So inventive invective won't get you disappeared. (U R.)

Or as that lyric hero, deep-sixed. The pure products of once-
grandeur,

Once public school eloquence, once-literate-America care not about words anymore:
Hatred is downloaded daily, right from those doing our imagining for us.

Fifth

Funny thing happened on my way to the mikvah—
In Salem, lost my chador, my chastity belt, my bad.

Please forgive the crash dummy, homey. No one thinks women are
Funny. But we have a driver's timing: even in the death seat.

Take my wife: a pole dancer in Krakow. She kills. Late night:
An actress playing Virginia Woolf with a rubber nose, to raves.

Honk honk! All wrong: our Virginia was a drop dead Groucho wit
Even as she filled her pockets with heavy stones and headed for it:

River of "Hello, I Must be Going," where death doubles back on itself.
Take my husband: how we met in Italy in the late Romantic style.

The night before I first saw his Mesmer face, I caught the shooting star,
Green & widening, arc of fire across the Tuscan sky—O look!

The gates keep opening on it: that lit-up, tear-filled, joke-black
City of Knock, knock: who's not? *Who's not? What then?*

Then, posthumous, the poet writes the world back into being.

TWIN CITIES III

Two cities: two minds & two
Languages perfect in their indifference

To each other. The one city where
Silence shoveled stone on stone.

The other city: voices successive
As gunfire. The shout & the echo

Of the shout heightened dialogue.
The ripped veil hung within a nun's cell,

My town's one marquee reading Tender &
Violent. You would fail accurately at describing

Your own life, certain as chance. His distance, his
Close-up, the child. Then all of it taken, unclaimed.

At the bedside of the couple: same betrayal,
Same loyalty. You will turn your back again,

The glass shattering. It was the one night hovering
By the blue shiftings of the pool—Love still trying to live,

Above, that weary star: reckless wish. Then the sudden
Twin—how she stepped out of me, took everything—

Then flung it back, whole, doubled, each time she turned
& turned, absorbed in breath, her task of never looking back.

ACKNOWLEDGMENTS

Thank you to my editor, Paul Slovak, for his steadfast and inspired loyalty to poetry and his wise insights in editing—and for making the Penguin Poets Series a welcome home for my poems.

All my love and gratitude to these dear friends who are my "home" in good times and bad: April Gornik, Eric Fischl, Dana Goodyear, Lt. Col. Edward Ledford, Lisa Russ Spaar, Elizabeth Bassine, Clare Rossini, Grace Schulman, Bob Holman, Nora Ephron, Susan Kinsolving, Diane Sokolow, Mona Simpson, Diane Luby Lane, Killarney Clary, Amy Schroeder, Janalynn Bliss, Jorie Graham, Mark Doty, Sophie Cabot Black, Lee Shallat Chemel, Swoosie Kurtz, Amy Theuninck, and John and Mary Lithgow. Here's a candle lit in the bank of votives—for Jason Shinder.

Grateful acknowledgement is made to the editors of the publications in which the poems in this book first appeared: *The Atlantic, The New Yorker, Alehouse, The American Poetry Review, The Paris Review, The Nation, The New York Times* Op-Ed Page, *Inkwell, The Chronicle of Higher Education, Upstreet, Verse Daily,* Slate, *Poetry Daily, Washington Square, Smartish Pace, Margie, Boston Review, The Kenyon Review,* and *Hunger Mountain.* **Some poems appeared in** *Poet's Alphabet,* **edited by David Young,** *New Poets of the American West,* **edited by Lowell Jaeger, and** *Dark Horses,* **edited by Joy Katz and Kevin Prufer.**

CARLOS PUMA

Carol Muske-Dukes is the award-winning author of seven books of poems, (the most recent, *Sparrow*, a National Book Award finalist) and four novels, plus two collections of essays and *Crossing State Lines: An American Renga*, co-edited with Bob Holman. She is currently poet laureate of the state of California and professor of English & Creative Writing at the University of Southern California, where she founded the Ph.D. program in Creative Writing & Literature. Her statewide poet laureate project is the Magic Poetry Bus. She reviews for *The New York Times*, *Los Angeles Times*, plus The Huffington Post. Her web site is www.carolmuskedukes.com.